Military Fighter Aircraft

by Grace Hansen

Abdo

MILITARY AIRCRAFT
& VEHICLES

Kids

abdopublishing.com

Published by Abdo Kids, a division of ABDO, PO Box 398166, Minneapolis, Minnesota 55439.

Printed in the United States of America, North Mankato, Minnesota.

102016

012017

THIS BOOK CONTAINS
RECYCLED MATERIALS

Photo Credits: af.mil, iStock, ©United States Government Work p.11,
©Jordan Tan p.22 / Shutterstock.com

Production Contributors: Teddy Borth, Jennie Forsberg, Grace Hansen

Design Contributors: Laura Mitchell, Dorothy Toth

Publisher's Cataloging in Publication Data

Names: Hansen, Grace, author.

Title: Military fighter aircraft / by Grace Hansen.

Description: Minneapolis, Minnesota : Abdo Kids, 2017 | Series: Military aircraft
    & vehicles | Includes bibliographical references and index.

Identifiers: LCCN 2016944090 | ISBN 9781680809350 (lib. bdg.) |
    ISBN 9781680796452 (ebook) | ISBN 9781680797121 (Read-to-me ebook)

Subjects: LCSH: Bombers--Juvenile literature. | Attack planes--Juvenile literature.
    | Airplanes, Military--Juvenile literature. | Fighter planes--Juvenile literature.

Classification: DDC 623.74--dc23

LC record available at http://lccn.loc.gov/2016944090

Table of Contents

Fighter Jets

Fighter jets are fast and easy to maneuver. They are meant for air-to-air combat. Their main purpose is to get airspace above battlefields.

F-16 Fighting Falcon

The F-16 Fighting Falcon is a multirole fighter. It is very good at fighting off enemy aircraft. But it can also attack enemies on the ground.

An F-16 can carry 6 air-to-air missiles, and much more. A cannon is built into the left wing. It can shoot 6,000 rounds per minute.

9

F-16s can fly 1,500 miles per hour (2,400 km/h)! **G-forces** are very hard for pilots to handle. Only the best pilots are chosen to fly F-16s.

F-22 Raptor

The F-22 Raptor excels in air-to-air combat. Its greatest strength is its **stealth**. Normal **radar** cannot detect this aircraft.

13

The F-22 carries six medium-range missiles. It also has two heat-seeking missiles. It can be armed with **smart bombs**.

14

The F-35 can fly many kinds of missions. It can fight air-to-air or air-to-ground. It is known for its **stealth**. So, it can also fly to gather **intelligence**.

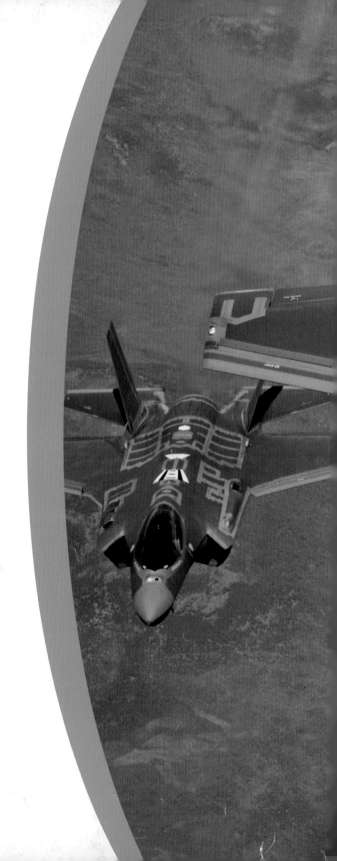

19

F-35 pilots wear a special helmet. They point their heads at the target. The plane locks onto the target and is ready to shoot.

WARNING - DO NOT CUT CANOPY
WITHIN 3 INCHES OF CANOPY FRAME

DANGER
EJECTION
SEAT
DANGER   DANGER

RESCUE

TURN FWD MASTER LATCH
AND AFT MASTER L
TO OPEN DOOR

CAUTION-HOT

CAUTION-HOT

FWD MASTER
LATCH (7/32 HEX)

AFT MASTER
LATCH (7/32 HEX)

5049

F-35 Lightning II Up Close

- Airspeed: 1,200 mph (1,931 km/h)
- Material absorbs **radar** waves
- Pratt & Whitney F135 Engine ------

- Internal weapons bays

Ceiling: 11+ miles (18.29+ km)

Range: 1,382 miles (2,224 km)

Glossary

G-force – the force of gravity.

intelligence – information about an enemy.

radar – a device for determining the presence and location of an object by measuring the time for the echo of a radio wave to return.

smart bomb – a steerable air-to-ground bomb that is guided to its target.

stealth – aircraft that is difficult to detect by sight, sound, radar, and infrared technology.

Index

abdokids.com

Use this code to log on to abdokids.com and access crafts, games, videos, and more!

Abdo Kids Code:
MMK9350